LOSING
A
MOTHER
LOSS, GRIEF AND HEALING

OSHIOKE ANAVBS

DEDICATION

This book is dedicated to God Almighty, my loving family and to all that have lost a parent. Most of all, I write this book to the memory of my mother, Elizabeth Izilein Anavbs. We love you.

ACKNOWLEDGMENT

I wish to credit all the images to VECTEEZY and others at CANVA. I am grateful to my father and my great cousin Itsegwe Ogbesor for their support.

TABLE OF CONTENTS

Chapter 1 - Loss and Grief

Loss is an unavoidable aspect of life. It is a feature of our human existence; it is unavoidable because everyone experiences it. It is a natural consequence of the fact that nothing lasts forever. Whether it be a loss of loved ones, a loss of property, or a loss of a dream, losing something that was once important to you can leave you feeling empty and lost.

It is important to remember that even though losing something may not feel good, it is also not the end of the world. Despite this, it is possible to come out of such experiences feeling stronger and more capable than before. No one knows what the future holds, so it's best to prepare yourself for anything. Learning to cope with loss is an essential part of life.

Often times, grief follows loss. Grief is just a natural element of the healing process, and this may come as a surprise to many of you. Grief can take many forms, and it is important to acknowledge your feelings. Whether it be anger, sadness, guilt, or a combination of these emotions, allowing yourself to feel them is essential to coping with the loss and moving forward.

There is no set timetable for grieving. Everyone has their own unique way of processing grief and healing, and it is important to recognize that. Although it can be excruciating at times, the grieving process should not be hurried. You must take the time to allow yourself to fully feel your emotions and express them so that you can eventually reach a place of acceptance and peace. It is important to be kind and gentle with yourself during this time.

Yes. Loss is an unavoidable part of life, but it is particularly difficult when a loved one dies, especially a mother. For me, the death of my mother was a shock that left me feeling numb and helpless.

I had treasured my mother's presence for the few years she had with us. The moments spent with her during her brief visits were lovely. The memories of these moments kept me going through the difficult days after she passed away. But then, in those early days of her loss, I was left alone and suddenly felt an unbearable emptiness. With my mother gone, I felt so isolated from the rest of the world. I was barely eleven, and her absence left a huge hole in my life as her first child.

There are numerous reasons for grief. These range from the death of a loved one to the loss of health due to a deadly illness. These are undoubtedly terrible times. But for me, the loss of my mother at such a young age was one of the most difficult events I have ever faced.

Coping with a severe loss can be one of the most trying moments in a person's life. Consider the death of a mother, who is one of the home's most important pillars.

Grieving over the loss of a mother, like I did, is by far the most painful loss one could go through. Mothers are said to be the glue that holds families together. They are the ones who communicate with all family members and spread love and goodness. They are typically the focal point of family life.

They arrange get-togethers and work tirelessly to keep the family together at home. When a mother dies, the family must either dissolve or find a replacement soon. The father cannot take her place as the family's primary communicator and organizer. Seriously.

Losing one's mother at any age is no laughing matter. That can be a terrifying experience. The loss could have come as a shock or could be the outcome of a mother's lengthy decline in health.

In both of these cases, having watched and experienced the process of losing a mother can be both physically and emotionally overwhelming. This could lead to a difficult time stabilizing or recovering from the traumatic incident.

Losing a mother can also create an immense sense of loneliness. This can be difficult to navigate. Your initial feeling of grief may be strong and closely followed by sadness. The impact of a mother's death can have an impact on your daily life, even years later.

It goes without saying that there is no set amount of time to mourn your mother's death. These feelings can often return and remain for years after the loss.

Whatever kind of loving relationship you had with your mother, losing her can be devastating. Be aware that help is always available. Many others, like you, have heartbreaking loss stories to tell, and I would like to share mine.

It was 1989, and I had just awoken from a terrifying night dream. To say it was a nightmare would be an understatement. I have had nightmares, but nothing as bizarre as this.

The sweat pouring from my brow as I awoke indicated that this was no ordinary dream. It did penetrate my entire subconscious. Because the terror manifested itself in the real world, to which I awoke. This dream had more of a tangible feel than any I had ever experienced before, and I was sure that it would remain embedded in my memory for some time.

I trudged along a well-known trail beneath the massive pillions on a dark and odd evening. I had just passed through a good friend's compound and was making my way around the curve to my house. My path was one of four that diverged from a road fork.

I became aware that the entire region was enveloped in yellow flames and ashes. It appeared to be a time for bush burning, as is customary for my people during the dry season. A desire for a rodent or bush kill drives teenagers to start such fires. This is true whether or not peasant farmers have cleaned the area around their farms to prevent fires from accidentally encroaching. Such fires burn extremely hot and rapidly spread.

A few yards down the road, I noticed a figure crouching and coated in ash. It had the appearance of a person. When I approached, the figure's hand moved, as if inviting me to pick it up. As I approached it to offer assistance, it transformed into a cleaned-out skeleton. I had no second thoughts and was suddenly on my way after picking up this skeleton. The skeleton felt oddly light as I held it in my arms, and as I looked around to see where I had stumbled upon this figure, I realized that the area was eerily silent. Everywhere I looked, it was empty and quiet, with no sign of any living being.

I had no idea what the skeleton meant, or why it had been there, but I knew that I was strangely compelled to take it with me. To my surprise, I had walked gleefully towards my family compound. The family was preparing supper for the evening and was rather animated behind the closed door of the kitchen barn. I hesitated for a second, wanting to surprise them with my new find, but I knew I had to seek my stepmother's consent first.

As I approached my stepmother and siblings, I was met with a blinding light. I offered to carry the skeleton into the barn, but my stepmother stopped me. I tried as many times as I could to persuade her of the importance of it and that it could be useful during my university days studying medicine.

Despite my attempts to explain to her why I needed the skeleton for my studies, she would not change her mind. She insisted that I drop it off outside. She had yelled at me to return it to where it came from. I was frustrated, but I did as she said. I am not sure how I eventually disposed of the skeleton because it left me and vanished as I joined them in the kitchen barn lights.

I had awoken sweating intensely from my dream. My heart was hammering as I peered across and around at my younger siblings, who were peacefully nestled away under the covers of their beds.

I did not tell anyone about the dream, but the clarity of all the objects in it all day was amazing. I spent the day puzzling over what it all meant and why I had seen such vivid imagery in a dream.

I went about my everyday activities as usual. The morning after the dream, I prepared and went to school. Afternoon arrived, and I and my siblings' lives were never the same again. On that day, we received the news of our mother's death.

My grandma, whom we have not seen since August of 1987, suddenly arrived that afternoon at our house. She had arrived with my younger sister by her side. Mother had taken us away from our father not long ago, in June of 1987.

We were only in elementary school when our mother left with us. She brought us back three months later and left us alone with our father and stepmother. We did not really understand the weight of her absence or what it would mean to not have her around, to not have her hugs, her cooking, and her love.

We were just excited that we were going to have a new adventure with our father. I remember we had dropped our bags and were glad to see Father again. We waved goodbye to our mother, not really understanding what was going on.

Hardly did we know that our mother would be gone in the next three years. We had been living with our father now, and he was a great father. Of course, it was a lot different than it had been with our mother around. Some privileges were cut off.

We were so young and naive that we did not understand that the love between mother and father had waned. To blame for it was the harsh economic situation back then under a stringent military government.

My father had lost his job a few years after the government came to power; my mother lost hers two years later. My parents had to resort to desperate measures in order to make ends meet, and this put a strain on their marriage. This ultimately resulted in their separating when I was a teenager. The lack of job security that the military government imposed on my parents not only affected their financial stability but also caused a strain on the livelihoods of many families back then.

There was a complete shift in dynamics at the hospital, and a lot of people had to be dropped. By now, the foreign doctors had all taken off back to their countries. Mr. and Mrs. Mathew had sent a telegram to us. They were back in India along with their friendly son and are all fine.

Dr. Demira almost left with my great cousin with the initial consent of my father, but a late change of heart stopped my cousin from going to China in the early years of 1985.

Mother was tired. She hated as we were going through a lot of suffering; hunger marked most of our days, and we barely had enough flesh on us. By providence, my cousin had taken a photo of us back then. Nobody would believe me if I told them I used to be as skinny. We were a sorry sight. It was no wonder my mother was moved by our suffering. She was mostly troubled by her incapability and regretted not being able to provide sufficiently for us. She could not take the negligee and cold treatment from her husband any longer.

We had spent about four months with her in her family residence in Ozalla, Owan, before she brought us back and remarried, settling alone away from her family ties.

She has paid us a few visits since then. She had missed us. My younger sister was with her at the time. My younger siblings and I stayed in Ozalla for four months before our mother took us back with her to start a new life away from her family.

Imagine my amazement when my grandma arrived with my younger sister. That day, I was happily preparing dinner in the kitchen barn when my grandma appeared out of nowhere, covering the entryway. What happened next surprised me. She burst into tears and turned away. I was caught off guard.

I suspected that a glance at what I was wearing had prompted her anguish. Is it possible that I appeared malnourished to her? My mind was racing with a million questions when I walked out of the kitchen. I didn't want to think about the possibility that my outfit could've had something to do with her reaction, so I shook off the thought and decided to keep it out of my head

I came to welcome my little sister. The excitement was great since she had packed her suitcase of clothes to signal a permanent stay with us. My little sister was standing in the center of the room, her suitcase of clothes signaling a permanent stay with us.

When I finally hugged her, I could feel all the years of longing for family time held in our embrace. I had asked why and how she had come to stay, but the fact that she had packed her suitcase of clothes was all that mattered.

I did not need to ask why or how; the fact that it was complete was all that mattered. My siblings were all back together.

The majority of grandma's time was spent with father. They talked for a while before she left. I had no idea that I would only have one chance to see her during my service year of 2004 before she died in 2014. I have always hoped that she died knowing that her grandchildren were doing well.

Living with the painful thought of her favorite grandkids in the absence of their mother would not have brought her serenity before her death. When she left, papa, who always maintains a cool manner, went about his daily routines. Nothing in his daily routine had altered.

I was sitting on the bed in our bedroom with my brothers and sister when suddenly my father walked in. He only approached us when it was dark in the evening. His facial expression was stern, and he had a serious look in his eyes. We knew something was wrong. We were huddled on our beds that night, discussing the evening's events.

Then my father cleared his throat and started speaking. He only added two sentences to the sound of his throat clearing. And that was it. That grandma had come to tell us some bad news: we had recently lost our mother. Period. He stood up and returned to his work.

"WRONG SWEEP"

"So dear was gentle she

That any walking gear

Stand not with glee

It was another wrong

Sweep of that coward's rake

Hoped not to claim a fake

But unfortunately the

Very best of our garden

On the worst moment

Of any hour

Had she made a will

Would have had it claimed still

I well remember the advice you gave

Little not knowing

I'll not behold you again

I still fight against losing bits of that angelic face

This threatens to blur, a nine year old ace

Could death but have a reason to drive?

A look over these nine-year dives

Through dawns of memories to save

Will jilt a shameful regret

For its unreasonable wave

This regardless arm of death

It's ever spinning wave of harvest

Picking the best from mother-earth."

#anavoshio

We exchanged glances for a moment before continuing our childish shouting and plays. It was as if the shock of the news had not hit us, or perhaps we simply wished to downplay it for the time being.

Who could blame us, who had never encountered death in our family? I was just eleven years old—the wisest and eldest. My younger sister was about three years old, my older brother was nine, and the others were seven and five.

"MY EARLY RIDE"

"If a seer had freely divined

My having an upper hand

Over this life from the hind

I bluntly would have denied

Tossing the barrage outside

To leave me but confide

In this simple life I will find

No warning signs given me

Death hid you from me

Forbidding permitting me

To hear your last for me

Patched sorts left me

Puzzling for a tiny frail me

Now alone, life ply on me

Street eyes eating into me

At every foot I tend to slide

As I take this early ride

Of responsibilities to grind."

#anavoshio

We were too young to understand the weight. I am sure we could cushion it because we would have been without our mother for over three years. When this happens to you, it is as if you have been "dropped from the skies into this new life with no instruction manual," as someone once stated.

To be honest, it is quite depressing. I was the only one who grew up remembering our mother fondly. My siblings have no recollection of her. We were a sorry bunch of delicate, innocent children. Left in the care of a distant and uncaring stepmother, we were unable to fill the void our mother left behind. We are to face the future with our stepmother and half-siblings. O my! And it was not a pleasant piggyback trip.

A woman's emotional intelligence and nurturing instincts are crucial in producing exceptional children. While there is no doubt that women may provide valuable guidance and support, the presence of a father is also essential to ensure the best outcome for the development of a child.

Without a father's involvement, children may lack the guidance needed to grow and thrive. Fathers can provide a unique form of support and guidance that builds character, resilience, and self-discipline. With both parents actively involved, their different perspectives and contributions give children a well-rounded experience that is invaluable as they become adults.

I am not suggesting that raising children without both parents is an impossible task or that those who do so are somehow inadequate, but research has demonstrated that the presence of both a mother and a father is associated with positive outcomes for children.

Fathers bring an important component to the parenting equation and are especially important in developing a child's confidence, sense of security, and moral compass. A father's presence can also help a child's emotional and social development.

It is not to say that women are unable to provide this level of support, but there are certain aspects of parenting that can only be provided by a father. Despite the indisputable advantages of having two parents, it is important to recognize that single-parent households have also had success raising healthy and productive members of society.

Not in every case, but there is always something missing in the lives of children raised by a single parent. For a healthy life experience and growth, children require both parents. A pair is always ideal.

Chapter 2 - Unwinding the Pains

My father had refused to tell me about my mother's death. All the while, I was troubled by what must have happened or the cause of her death. This was hidden from me until we arrived at an aunt's house in Benin City in the rainy season of 1991.

Father and I had traveled to Benin City, the state capital, to prepare for my admission to the newly established government model schools. Father stopped at one of my aunt's houses before we left Benin City for Auchi, our home, that day.

My great cousin was also present. This relative of mine was literally brought up by my father and mother.

So he was my big brother growing up in the opulent mixed staff quarters of the now-defunct SAGGS, Jattu, which shared a boundary with the small village of Afashio, Uzairue.

When my cousin and I sat outside, father was having a good time with them inside the house. I told him about his mother's death and the dream I had before my maternal grandma delivered the dreadful news that day.

He dashed inside to tell my father how surprised he was. Then he told my father about my dream. My father just opened up after that. He told him the exact cause of my mother's death and the events that followed. Mother had perished in an inferno. The hidden cause and the hidden aftermath kept from me all these years are really gory to describe here. It was no wonder, my father had guarded us, her offspring, from knowing the truth. I've kept these secrets from my siblings for 33 years. As they say, like father, like son.

After being admitted to the prestigious school, I was named pioneer class sanitary and health prefect. By the second year, my academic performance and behavior had earned me the position of senior prefect. I performed my duties admirably and held this position of leadership till we graduated five years later.

While we were in third grade, I had a minor squabble with the school driver, Mr. Ajax, who threw away my bucket before I could obtain water from the school water truck. Being the senior prefect at the time, I did not expect to be treated that harshly. I took my bucket quietly and went straight to bed. Then the unexpected happened.

This was a watershed moment in my life since it was the first time I sobbed over the loss of my mother. It shocked me that it took me four years to cry over the loss of my precious mother. The pain of the loss was so fresh and, at the same time, devastating. Despite the sadness I felt, I eventually came to terms with her death, something that I didn't think was possible before that moment. The experience taught me the importance of grieving and how to allow myself to feel the emotions associated with loss.

"PASSING AWAY"

"I had asked once again
Yes, I had asked the divine
That same question
To which I needed answers
To save me from pains
Of being left alone in this world
In this cold heartless world
As I broke down and cried
Alone again and again."
#anavoshio

All of her memories came flooding back with amazing intensity. The agony was excruciating. I cried on my bed that night like I had never cried before in my life.

Keeping the pains and losses bottled up for so long sapped my strength. I felt a mixture of rage and love for her for leaving us at such a young age.

The agonies I had endured over the years from my stepmother, who was determined to eliminate us by any means, came flooding back to me. I screamed angrily.

Sometimes we miss the mothers we hoped we had more than the mothers we had. My rage that night was directed towards my mother. I blamed her for my misfortunes at the hands of my stepmother and those who sought to crush the little us.

I cried out to God, asking why mother had not been there for us all these years. As I watched others and their mothers carry on with zeal and the love and adoration they shared, I felt envious.

It was the overwhelming sensation I had when I broke down. There was a deep sense of regret and pain that if my mother had been alive, I would not have had to endure all of my hardships and misfortunes.

This wrath was so vivid and intense that it might literally set a curtain on fire. I'm joking. Nonetheless, it is excruciatingly painful, tearing at the heart.

Denying your feelings may appear to be a faster way to heal. You may also get the impression that others want you to bury your grief and move on before you have fully accepted your loss.

I must remind you that grieving is a difficult and painful process. You should not be discouraged by the opinions of others.

Some people heal through their grief quickly and move on, keeping the traces of their anguish carefully hidden away. As I did. Others, regardless of how predictable the death was, require more time and assistance.

The length of the grieving process varies from person to person. It is critical to be gentle with yourself as you go through each of your individual reactions to the loss. Things normally get better with time and assistance, I must say.

Mothers have given us so much. Many of us would not be where we are today if it were not for them. That kind of connection is 98% irreplaceable.

I have very early memories of mother. Every family photo and all the fuse around them have never escaped my memory. I clearly can recall every event surrounding any family photo taken back then. I can also recall being the first to go grabbing hold of mother food flask when she arrived from work at the hospital.

Mothers nurse uniform was always prime and adoring. She was full of elegance when dressed for work. The hospital shares a boundary with the school my father works.

We all lived in the staff residential quarters with other foreign nationals. Mr. and Mrs. Mathew, the Indians. They both handled the staff quarter's children every Sunday in what was called a Children's Sunday school.

The little every Sunday candy sweets gifts were enough to keep us ever punctual and disciplined. The every year Children Anniversary was super. Here, I had played my first acting role and met some pretty dark skinned Indian ladies my age. We were all very shy back then. Surprising I still have my lines in the mini dramas in my head to this day.

There was Dr. Demira, the Chinese and Dr. Stevenson, the Briton and Dr. Thomas who were in the doctor's quarters. I cannot forget how mother would grip me like a lamb before slaughter else I would sprint off even when seriously ill from taking an injection. I just hated needles. My, my! Even till date.

There were black workers over there too. Living with everyone peacefully for the sweet few early years of mine was a memorable one. And watching and nurturing us was one I grew to regard as a super Mother, strong and multi-talented. Guess most children see their mothers in the same limelight.

Chapter 3 - Life without Mother

This week marks the 33rd anniversary of my mother's death. It would be an understatement to say we were close. You will see what a small precious gem I was to her as the first fruit of her labor pangs.

"LOVING MUM"

"Destined first to be lain

The first fruit of your labor pain

You had welcomed me though spent

A human so small but a saint

A cry from my cradle bed
And you were over me like a bird
Towering above me with your nursing eyes
Watching over my little size

Could any be like you?
Guess, only a scarcely few
As I recalled looking around at birth
To find tender love here on earth
Would mean a long wait
For smiles showered on
Surprised my wails taken for fun."
#anavoshio

I do not know what it was, but my stepmother was
bent on eliminating us. On a Sunday afternoon when
she thought no one was in the room, I overheard her
telling a close friend and confidant over the window.

"If not for the love their father has for them, I would
have had them poisoned all along." She swore.

This was coming from a lady who has six female children of her own. Could it be because of my mother's male dominance over her? What inheritance does she seem to fight over, and why was she so bent on evil and hatred?

My younger brother was beaten up by her once for no apparent reason or offense. I felt so helpless, but I was determined to do something about it. I knew I had to challenge her.

So, I took a deep breath and faced her. I was terrified, but I mustered up the courage to speak up and ask her why she had to lay her hands on my younger one.

She looked at me with anger in her eyes, ready to fight back with all her fury. I held my ground, standing still and maintaining eye contact with her as I waited for her response.

All of a sudden, she rushed at me with all her strength and almost knocked me off balance where I stood. She was shocked that I did not fall over from her weight. Then the fight started.

My resilience helped me grow bolder and more courageous during the fight. I just discovered I had really grown big and strong to defend my siblings from her taunting routines.

Anyway, I did not escape being bitten close to my left eye during the fight. She had meant to blind me outright. To leave a mark on me and make me not forget, she was not to be challenged, ever.

She seemed to realize after the fight that this would never happen for the weak kids she once knew who had died. Now they just proved they could revolt.

Father had only come out to console me. He applied a balm to the bite area. It was very close to the eye. Her gripping teeth would have turned my eyeball to pulp in an inch. After the fight, he seemed not to have taken sides. She was warned not to repeat it ever again.

School the next morning saw me with a heavy eyelid. I lied to my friends that it was a bee sting to cover up the shame that a woman did it to me. At least to save me a mock-free life.

My stepmother never threatened me after that. Never again. But, as of the time I became a border guard at Olona, only God knows what my siblings who remained behind faced from her.

The first year as a border was a stressful and family-struggling one. It was the first time I realized there was peace outside of my home. I was so at peace at the boarding school that the midterm break

In my second year, I stayed back at school as my friends took off with their parents for the holiday. I just did not want the drama that I always met back home during holidays then.

Noticing my staying behind for the holidays, a few students, mostly juniors, whose homes were close by, stayed back with me for company.

And so started the trend of students staying back for midterm breaks until I graduated from the prestigious secondary school.

On reaching home after graduation, I was given food by my stepmother. Only that it was the last free food we ever got from her. She literally stopped feeding me and my siblings after that day.

Whether to signal that now that you've finished school, you should get a job and fend for yourselves I really did not have a clue. But it was a warning sign to get things established immediately; otherwise, we will go hungry henceforth.

My first paying job was a hire to train some adults for an upcoming national examination, and the pay was enticing. So I took up any school tutoring job I could find and made my teaching talent famous.

Everyone wanted to relate to and get a drink from this young, bright kid on the block. Thanks to Onicha-Olona for the training and teaching. I am forever indebted to that place and her teachers. God bless them.

I got my first non-school job at a factory in Aviele, Alims Plastic Factory in the next town. We operated in shifts. Robosky, a childhood friend, was there to guide me and keep me company. He has been there now for three years and is not doing badly.

He was moved to a higher section due to his diligence and quick reflexes. During my stay at the factory, I made new friends and learned a lot of life-changing lessons.

I had to take the job because of the higher pay. I still kept one of the teaching jobs, where I home tutored one of the polytechnic lecturer's children. I remember the plastic company truck picking us up at the various spots in town.

The night shift was peaceful and tidy. I met lady Akuet during one of these shifts. I was a naive kid back then. I just could not really see the affection and crush most of the ladies had on me. I just smiled along and that was all.

The disturbing situation back home with my little siblings was enough of a distraction for me for many years to come. I could not establish a deep female relationship just yet.

It was really a moment in time in my history of working as a teenager. My family was going through a tough economic crisis, and I had to help my siblings get through it, being the eldest.

Working at the factory was initially hard and grueling, but the money I earned gave us our first television, a radio-cassette player, and for me, my first much-needed pair of shoes in years.

One day during work, there was an accident, and my hand was caught in the sealing machine. A quick save from Robosky, and my hand would have been badly injured. After this incidence, my plans to go back to school became intensified. I have to go back to school.

It is so painful and draining to work as hard as a teenager could to care for my younger siblings. It was an incredibly difficult situation to be in, but it was admirable that I took on such a responsibility at such a young age.

I learned a lot and developed skills that have remained with me. It was not a problem blending into the harsher northern region of the country for a job and excelling where others had failed.

My sadness at my mother's death was complicated. It had always puzzled me throughout the years. Important dates, holidays, and other reminders have also taken their toll on me, evoking sorrowful thoughts associated with her death.

The majority of them were turned into sorrowful mother poems and ballads in my published poem collection on Amazon.

The sadness and disappointment we feel when we are unable to see our parents express their grief over their deaths We are mourning the loss of things like celebrating birthdays together, cooking for one another, gathering at restaurants for family meals, sharing hugs, and walking hand in hand.

How do you manage life without your mother? How does one manage a lifeline after losing a parent? Loss is a very personal experience, and only you know what is important to you.

Humans frequently link particular losses with intense grief. The loss of a close friend, lover, family member, or classmate is one example. Grief might be triggered by a loved one's grave illness or even from an emotional breakup. At these moments, taking care of yourself, getting support, and acknowledging your feelings can all help you deal.

Self-validation is one method of coping with sadness. What exactly is "self-validation"? Encouragement, appreciating your strengths, triumphs, progress, and effort, identifying and embracing your feelings, prioritizing your needs, treating yourself with compassion, saying lovely things to yourself, and accepting your limitations, defects, and mistakes are all examples of self-validation.

Do not engage in self-judging, self-criticism, or comparisons with others. Rejecting your needs and feelings, practicing perfectionism, and harshly judging oneself are not healthy ways of validating yourself.

It did not deprive me of any method of dealing with my pain. It is natural to be sad, afraid, furious, or lonely right now.

Recognizing these emotions can be really beneficial. Looking at these mourning sentiments is highly informative and helpful in explaining the physiological impacts on sleep, appetite, energy level, and motivated attitude of a bereaved person, especially if the loss is painful, such as the loss of a mother.

I must have unwittingly used a tactic that was already ingrained in me. My family was quite close.

There is no connection to the outside world. Even among relatives, it was lightly tolerated.

My father was a strong father figure in my life. He sets a standard for you and encourages you to achieve your goals.

You will never hear him moan or see him faint. My father can never be overburdened with secrets. That is a proven fact.

The world cannot shake his determination. This is something I have seen throughout the years. It was as if he had been prepared for any eventuality. Because he always manages to solve even the most difficult problems in a straightforward manner. Could I have learned from him while I locked up my sadness for years? Perhaps.

I learned that self-validation is a learned ability. As you become more adept at validating yourself, you will seek less external validation and be less tolerant of others invalidating you.

You must pay attention to how you feel and what you require. Then you must accept your emotions and wants without judgment.

When you are feeling down, gather positive attitudes. Do not identify too strongly with your emotions. We want to acknowledge our emotions while also remembering that they do not define us.

I may have merely glanced at my siblings when I learned of my mother's death, but my thoughts were elsewhere.

Several affirmative statements were racing through my little mind. I believe such a feeling is normal. My emotions were normal. That was difficult, but I knew I could do it.

What do we require in order to cope or feel better? Is it acceptable not to cry? Should I act as if I am not bothered? These are not healthy ways to deal with grief after a loss. Losses can elicit intense emotions of grief.

Those around you may not know the extent of your feelings, but let your feelings out. Do not be ashamed. Others around you may not understand the depth of your emotions, but they express them. Do not be embarrassed.

We are burdened by the grief of having lost our beloved mothers; this is a loss we all share. Life, nevertheless, must carry on.

Chapter 4 - Types and Coping with Losses

TYPES OF LOSSES

Sudden losses caused by events such as accidents or suicide can be distressing. In this unpredictable world, there is no way to prepare for this. Hey! It should be noted that miracles do exist and can completely alter your thoughts and predictions.

In any case, an unexpected loss might shake your sense of security and confidence in the regularity of life.

As a result, you may have symptoms such as sleep difficulty, nightmares, upsetting thoughts, a sad mood, social isolation, or extreme anxiety.

All of these are ways your body is attempting to repair or adjust after a traumatic incident.

Predictable losses, such as those caused by terminal illness, might sometimes provide more time to prepare for the eventual aftermath.

The downside is the pain associated with the loss's expectation and the grief associated with the loss itself.

In my instance, I was completely unprepared. It was an unexpected loss on our part. We had all assumed she was going about her everyday chores in a healthy manner.

If my mother ever had a medical problem, I never saw her suffer from one during the ten years I had her in my life. I wish I were so fit and healthy.

Do men and women handle losses in the same way? According to a 2007 study by Trusted Source, the death of a mother has a more detrimental impact on daughters than on sons.

According to the study, women who have lost a mother are more likely than men to binge drink, have a lower level of self-esteem, and have a lower degree of personal progress.

A 2015 study discovered that when a parent dies, women experience a more profound grieving response and have more trouble adjusting to the loss.

The death of a loved one can seem unreal, especially when it happens to a parent. This is someone whose presence in your life may have been constant.

You had finished growing up and had achieved adulthood, yet you still needed your parents' comfort in your life.

It might be difficult to grieve the loss of their compassionate support, counsel, and affection. It produces a tremendous void and pain that may appear insurmountable. The outer world may expect you to recover swiftly from your sadness.

You may be granted a five-day mourning leave for the loss, as well as a few extra days of personal time, before returning to work abruptly. The world around you may believe that life continues on, but have you?

COPING WITH LOSSES

Every one of us has a unique way of dealing with difficult situations. Several people have different approaches to dealing with their losses.

Everyone will go through their own sorrow journey in their own unique way. Some people may need more time than others to adequately grieve the loss of a loved one.

Grief feelings may come and go, with the degree of sadness fluctuating at different periods. This can make it difficult to feel like you have made any progress with your grieving.

It is possible that you will feel better for a while, only to have your grief resurface. This is typical. Some people may discover that their grief is exacerbated around holidays or other significant dates.

The ache of mourning may reduce with time, but it is still possible to remain emotionally connected to someone who has died for many years.

Sorrow after the death of a parent can drain you and leave you reeling, regardless of the type of relationship you had.

Understand that grieving is a natural, healthy process that takes different forms for different people. Treat yourself with warmth and compassion, and embrace patience as you move through your grief.

Talking to friends who have experienced loss in the past can help you develop fresh coping strategies. Only you know what suits your personality and lifestyle the best.

One method to analyze your own coping style is to recall how you dealt with difficult situations in the past. It is crucial to note that some methods of coping with loss, such as talking to others or writing in a journal, can be beneficial.

Others may be harmful or damaging to the healing process, such as substance abuse or isolation. Good coping skills are essential for addressing a loss and moving ahead in the healing process.

There is no correct or incorrect way to grieve the death of a parent. Some people will be sad or despondent, while others will be offended or angry at the departed, themselves, others, or even higher forces.

That was my situation. I recall wondering why this had to happen to us when we were so young. I was the only child, and I was old enough to comprehend the situation. I was upset and worried that if I acted out to express my emotions, I would be misinterpreted. I am sure my father would chastise me for that.

Some people may have felt worry, anxiousness, or fearfulness, as well as guilt or remorse. I would rather be ambivalent, numb to the true events going on around me. It is something I know my father would appreciate. He would not want to see me drained of energy and ambition to keep going for the sake of my younger siblings.

Did I perceive grieving as a healing process? Yes. It is vital to emphasize that the grief process is not a straight line but rather a series of highs and lows.

Sorrow is sometimes considered to be accelerated, but nature cannot be fooled. The smaller the weight and the less impact it has on your daily life, the more confident you are that you are making progress.

Being patient with the process and allowing yourself to experience any sensations associated with the loss might be beneficial. Talking to a counselor or a supportive person may help you move forward in the healing process if you feel stuck in your grief.

Your cultural background can influence how you interpret and approach loss. Some cultures expect a period of mourning and have established rituals to assist people in the grieving process.

Mourning rituals and ceremonies honor loss while also providing social support and reaffirming life.

You may be unaware of how your cultural background influences your grieving process. One strategy to increase your awareness of potential cultural effects in your life is to talk with family, friends, or clergy.

Friends and family members may be able to assist you in coming up with ideas for your own traditions.

Chapter 5 - Stages and Support

THE STAGES OF GRIEF

Be aware that emotions can shift. You may experience a range of emotions and feelings in the days, weeks, and months following the death of a parent. They may change over time as well.

Some people may experience what is known as the "five stages of grieving." These are some examples.

The first stage of grief is denial. People often feel shocked and confused in the wake of the death of a parent, making it hard to process the reality of their loss. In this stage, they may try to keep themselves busy and distracted, using any means necessary to avoid confronting their grief.

As a coping mechanism, denial can be a way of protecting oneself from the intensity of the emotional pain associated with the loss. However, it is important to recognize that this is just a temporary solution, and that ultimately the bereaved must go through the grieving process in order to heal.

The second stage of the grief process is rage. During this stage, a person may be overcome with feelings of annoyance, rage, and resentment. This can manifest itself in the form of impatient, sarcastic, or gloomy behavior.

In some cases, individuals may even turn to substance abuse or engage in physical altercations as a form of venting or as a means of expressing their frustration. In addition to these possible reactions, a person may also feel overwhelmed by their emotions and lash out in ways that are uncharacteristic of their normal behavior.

It is important to remember that these feelings of anger and hostility are a normal part of the grieving process, and should not be suppressed.

The third stage of grief is the negotiation phase. During this time, individuals may experience a range of emotions that are often intense, ranging from shame and guilt to blame and insecurity.

In this stage, individuals may reflect longingly on the past or worry about the future. They may also pass judgment on themselves and/or others, become overly analytical, and become consumed with concerns.

Additionally, individuals may explore the possibility of faith, spiritualism, and/or other forms of healing in hopes of finding comfort and closure.

It is important to note that the negotiation phase of grief is often the longest stage, and it is crucial to seek support and practice self-care while navigating these emotions.

Depression is the fourth stage of grief and is considered the most difficult. People may feel a wide range of intense emotions during this stage, such as hopelessness, unhappiness, disappointment, and overwhelming sadness.

Other physical signs of depression may also be present, such as changes in sleep or eating habits, a loss of interest in social activities, and a general lack of vitality.

It is important to note that everyone experiences grief differently, and depression should not be seen as an unnatural or abnormal reaction. The reduced levels of energy can be further compounded by a lack of concentration, difficulty in making decisions, and suicidal thoughts.

It is important to seek help from a qualified mental health professional if depression symptoms are prolonged or severely impactful.

At the fifth and final stage of sorrow, acceptance is reached. People may start to feel self-compassion, strength, pride, and even wisdom. This can also bring about a sense of pride, as individuals may recognize their resilience and ability to cope.

In some cases, there may be a wisdom that is gained from the experience, allowing individuals to gain insight into the process of grief and to reflect on their personal journey.

They can accept the reality of the situation for what it is and be present in the moment, allowing them to adjust and cope with whatever is happening. People may start to gain a greater understanding of themselves, their situation, and the world around them.

This can lead to a newfound appreciation for life and the strength to carry on. It can also give them the courage to make reparative changes.

Acceptance is an important stage in the grief process, and can offer people the opportunity to regain control, look ahead, and move forward with their lives.

SUPPORTING THOSE GRIEVING

Once the shock of the loss wears off, the griever's feelings of anguish and melancholy intensify.

Well-meaning friends may avoid discussing the matter because they are uncomfortable with their own pain or are afraid of making the individual feel awful. As a result, grieving people frequently feel more alienated or lonely in their mourning.

Individuals who are mourning are prone to alternate between wanting times alone and wanting to be near others. They might wish to chat with someone about their feelings.

Simply be a good listener. While you sit with them, inquire about their emotions. If you have had similar life situations, now is the time to express yourself. Be really close to their intuitions and let them feel free to express themselves to any extent.

Inquire about their loss. Make them believe that acknowledging the suffering is a good thing in order to move on. Let them be sad, since it is unwise to reduce or avoid grief. Make yourself available when possible and discuss your personal losses. Realize that your feelings are valid.

Grief is frequent after the death of a parent, but other emotions are also normal. You may not feel sad, and that is just fine. Maybe you are just numb or grateful they are no longer in pain.

Sorrow unleashes a torrent of nuanced, often conflicting feelings. Your connection with your parents may have been difficult, but it was still a vital part of your identity. They either made you or chose to adopt and nurture you, becoming your first anchor in the world.

It is common to struggle or encounter difficulty coming to grips with your grief after such a huge loss. You may feel rage or resentment, as well as shame for not contacting them frequently or being present at their death.

Some people may feel shocked and emotionally numb, while others may suffer from uncertainty, disbelief, or a sense of unreality.

They are accompanied by feelings of hopelessness or despair, bodily pain, mental health symptoms such as depression or suicidal tendencies, and a sense of relief.

No matter how the loss affects you, remember that your feelings are valid, even if they differ from what others expect you to feel. Let yourself truly experience the loss, regardless of how long it takes.

Individuals react to sorrow in various ways, but it is critical to allow yourself to feel all of your emotions.

There is no single correct method to grieve, no specific period of time after which you should expect to feel better, and no stages or procedures to cross off a checklist. This can be difficult to accept on its own. Consider that.

If your mother died after a protracted illness, you may have had more time to prepare, but no amount of planning will make your loss any less intense when it arrives. You may still be startled and disbelieving, especially if you hoped for their recovery right up until the end.

On the other hand, the untimely loss of a mother in her forties may cause you to confront your own mortality, which can further compound your sorrow.

Chapter 6 - Impact and the Therapist

IMPACT OF GRIEF

The impacts of sorrow can have a profound effect on one's daily life and mental state. Feelings of sorrow can come on suddenly and without warning, leaving the individual feeling overwhelmed and out of sorts.

The emotional intensity of sorrow can interfere with an individual's daily activities, leading to difficulty in concentrating, sleeping, and feeling motivated.

Furthermore, during times of sorrow, an individual may experience a profound sense of loneliness and isolation, leading to further emotional distress. It is important to remember that, although sorrow is a difficult emotion to experience, it is a necessary part of life and can provide valuable insight into how we are feeling.

Everyone experiences sorrow differently and it is important to find ways to recognize and cope with it in a healthy way.

Additionally, those struggling with depression have a wide range of therapeutic options, such as cognitive-behavioral therapy, psychotherapy, and medication, which can be discussed with a mental health provider

You may experience sleep issues, an increase or decrease in appetite, irritability, poor concentration, or increased alcohol or substance usage. You may find it difficult to work, care for your household, or meet your own basic needs.

The necessity of finalizing your parent's affairs may overwhelm you, especially if you must do so alone. You can also talk to your peers about your concerns.

"THE WILL"

"Not even much was left for choice
As they scrambled for her asset
Which they knew no course
Leaving behind me no relics to fret

And to add they'd all lied to me
Each playing so false a part
All for softening my heart to tin
With stories so widely apart

Peace be unto them as long as I bear my flesh
I'll ever dauntingly tarry to bare minds
That she's alive and fresh
With the angels in the clouds."
#anavoshio

The task of finalizing your parent's affairs can be a daunting one, particularly if you are doing it alone. It is important to remember that you are not alone in this process and that there are resources available to you.

You can reach out to your peers or other individuals who have experienced similar difficulties in the past, to talk about your concerns and feelings. Connecting with others who are in the same situation may help you to feel less isolated, and provide you with a valuable support system as you go through this process.

Additionally, you can also seek out professional advice from an experienced attorney and financial advisor who can help you to understand the legal and financial ramifications of the situation. Being well informed during times of transition can also be beneficial. They can provide guidance and support as you navigate the unique challenges of the situation.

Some people find solace in the distraction of work, but if at all possible, avoid forcing yourself to return before you are ready. To escape the ever-present wall of painful emotions, people frequently immerse themselves in work, taking on more than they can comfortably bear.

It is important to remember that grief is a natural response to difficult times and it is only a temporary experience. Although we don't know when the current circumstances will come to an end, we can be sure that it is not a sustainable way of life.

Grief is a necessary process that can help us to cope with difficult situations and ultimately lead to healing. It is important to recognize that it is ok to feel overwhelmed by the current challenges and to give oneself permission to process the emotions that come with it. Doing so can help us to find the strength to move forward, even in the most uncertain of times.

It is also important to take the necessary steps to cope with your grief during this time, such as speaking to a professional therapist or counselor. By taking the proactive steps to manage your feelings, you can find a sense of peace and comfort in the midst of difficult times.

TALKING TO A THERAPIST

There is no shame in needing further assistance as you begin to process your parent's loss. In fact, many counsellors specialize in grief counselling.

A therapist can provide validation and direction as you begin to move through the complex emotions that often accompany grieving. Grief counsellors can also offer you coping methods to help you adjust to life without your parents.

Counselling also provides a safe environment to process any guilt, anger, resentment, or other remaining feelings associated with a deceased parent's poisonous or cruel behavior, as well as to gain some sort of closure.

A therapist can offer empathetic help if you wish to forgive your parent but do not know where to start. Speak with a professional.

After a major loss like this, therapy might be beneficial. While most therapists have worked with sorrow because it is one of the most common life experiences, there are some who specialize in working with clients who are grieving. To locate one, look for a grief therapist or a grief counsellor in your neighborhood.

Nevertheless, if you have never discussed or processed what happened, you may find it even more difficult to grieve and move on after their passing. Speaking out to a therapist or someone you trust can help ease the burden.

Grief Support Groups: While friends and loved ones can provide solace, a grief support group can meet a different type of social need by connecting you with others who have suffered similar losses.

It is normal to be upset or frustrated when individuals in your life who have not experienced loss try to console you or offer concern.

They simply do not understand what you are going through, no matter how polite or well-intended their remarks are.

In a support group, you might find common ground and validation for emotions that you are unable to communicate to others.

A 2021 study discovered that parental loss is associated with depression and a weakened sense of self in young adults.

The Diagnostic and Statistical Manual of Mental Disorders (5th ed.), a reference tool used by mental healthcare practitioners, lists a variety of normal emotions experienced in the year following parental bereavement. Regret, remorse, worry, guilt, emptiness, rage, anger, grief, and numbness are examples of these sentiments.

Losing your mother can have far-reaching consequences. You may feel as if you have lost a vital component of your support network. You may be saddened by the loss of family traditions and cultural knowledge.

You may also notice that your family relationships have become strained. Siblings and other parental figures may seem far away. They may require their own time to grieve, or they may not be as emotionally available as your mother was.

Everyone experiences grief differently after the death of a mother. Grief that interferes with daily functioning or lasts more than a year may necessitate the assistance of a mental health professional.

Chapter 7: Managing Your Inner Strength

HONORING THEIR MEMORIES

Many people believe that specific actions might help honor and console a deceased parent. Sharing recollections and anecdotes with family members and other loved ones about what your parent meant to you can help keep their memory alive.

If you have children, you may tell them stories about their grandparents or carry on family customs from your upbringing.

It may be unpleasant to recall at first, but you may find that your sadness begins to ease as the memories begin to flow.

If you are unable to openly discuss your parent's death at this time, collecting images of wonderful times or writing them a letter expressing your grief over their death will assist.

Of course, not everyone has fond memories of their parents. Individuals frequently avoid expressing negative memories of deceased loved ones. If they abused, neglected, or wounded you in any way, you may wonder if it is worth bringing up old wounds.

You may make a little house tribute with photos and memorabilia, or you could plant their favorite tree or flower in your backyard. Others do;

Cook Something: Channeling your mother's cooking abilities is a terrific way to feel closer to her while also enjoying a delicious dinner.

Print a picture of you and your mother when you were babies and display it on your table or wallet. Put up pictures of you and your mother on the walls to give her the attention she deserves.

Check out this cool video: Looking at family photos and videos can be healing. It acts as a healthy getaway to joyous moments in our lives by reminding us of the fantastic experiences we have had together. It keeps those memories alive in our minds and fosters thankfulness. We reduce worry as we enhance our gratitude.

Frequent Check-Ins: It's important to establish a relationship with your parents, especially if they live alone. It can be difficult to get in touch with them when they live far away and you may not know what their schedule is like. Regular check-ins can help ensure that you stay in contact with them. If you're worried about them, it's easy to set up an app for them on your phone that will alert you when they are nearby. Even after they have left us, they have always been a part of us, so we should continue to honor them, especially mothers.

Nothing on this planet can ever truly replace her. We love you and appreciate everything you have done for us, mothers everywhere.

Allow others to comfort you: You and your friends and loved ones may be at a loss for words if they have not experienced the same type of loss. It is true that their presence can make you feel less alone.

It is natural to need time to mourn quietly, but entirely isolating yourself usually does not help. The company and support of those closest to you can help you cope with your loss.

Beyond giving a supportive presence, friends can also help out with food, child care, or handling errands.

Speak Up: Simply inform them of your needs. You may invite them to join you in a distracting activity, such as playing a game, watching a movie, or working on a house project.

Accept Family Relationships: After your parent's death, you may discover that family connections begin to shift. If your remaining parent is still alive, he or she may now turn to you and your siblings for assistance.

Your siblings, if you have any, are going through the same thing. Because of their particular bond with your parent, they may experience the loss differently than you.

It is fairly uncommon for siblings to disagree or gradually grow apart, especially if you disagreed on your parent's end-of-life care.

Yet, family ties can give solace during times of sadness. You have all suffered the same loss, even though that individual meant different things to each of you.

Make an effort to strengthen and draw closer to your family relationships if you value them.

This could imply reaching out more frequently than in the past or inviting those who visit and participate in family events more frequently.

It can also imply listening with empathy when a sibling who had a tough connection with your mother is now struggling to cope with contradictory emotions.

UNCOVERING INNER STRENGTH

Take care of yourself.

The effects of grief can be felt in a variety of ways. Sleep deprivation, a low appetite, and a weakened immune system are all common symptoms. The treatment is intended to protect your health and fitness. Start walking with a companion, eat natural, unprocessed food, and remain hydrated. When your body feels powerful, it will raise your mood and help you deal.

Pardon yourself.

When a parent dies, shame can become a burden due to prior disputes that you now regret or because you believe you did not do enough to aid them. You must understand that no parent-child relationship is ever ideal. Even if you were rarely told, you were still loved. Please dwell on the positive times instead. The good old days are what they want you to remember.

Take a break.

Resting after funeral arrangements and legal concerns is essential for your physical and mental health. It's important to take a break and rest. It's hard to think about what will happen next, and your mind will be going in all different directions. It's important to take some time for yourself and make sure you're not just trying to get through the day.

You might feel like you're not doing anything, but it's just as important to take care of your mental health as it is your physical health. If you take a trip to recover when things have calmed down, you will be able to return invigorated to aid your family in the long run. Never feel bad about taking time off from your usual routine or work.

Cherish valuable memories.
I learned that by remembering the pleasant times we had, I could still enjoy my mother's company. Do not prevent yourself from mentally recalling your valuable experiences. A time will come when you will smile or chuckle to yourself just as you did at the time. So keep your mother in your thoughts.

Have patience.
It's natural to miss a parent as you grow up, but if you were close to them, you will need time to adjust. It may be hard to imagine life without your parents, but you will find that it is easier to live life with them gone.

You will learn that it is important to go out and experience life by yourself, and it is important to remember the good memories of your parents. Do not wish away time with the intention of hastening the healing process. The recovery process will proceed at its own natural speed.

Accept the new you.

As we get older, our opinions and attitudes toward life can change. One of those life-changing events is the death of a mother or parent. Sorrow heightens awareness that everything changes, so prioritize what is truly important. Cherish and enjoy each waking minute, and let the new you seize each precious day with zeal.

Resist making analogies.

During grieving, there is no such thing as a person who is not affected by grief. There is no right or wrong way to grieve, so do not pass judgment on your response to loss. You are not required to look or act a certain way. Do not be concerned about how it appears to others or what they may think. This is your own particular adventure.

Uncovering a New Chapter

The death of a parent is frequently dismissed by society as a natural course of events, but those who have experienced it understand how life-changing it is. You feel pain and loss because you have a heart, but your heart is stronger than you could have thought. Life exists to be loved.

Assist your families.

The passing of a parent can send a tremor across the whole family. We may shrink in our sadness and fail to notice that others are also grieving. After the loss of your mother, you may feel like you have nothing to live for.

However, it is important to take the time to help other family members that are still alive. There are many ways to help out your family members. One way is to help them with their chores. For example, if you have a sibling who has a child, help them do their chores. When they are done, they will be able to spend more time with their child and you will be able to get more time with your sibling.

Another way to help out is by going grocery shopping for your family members. This can also give you time to talk about what happened with your mother.

GRIEF MANAGEMENT

There is nothing that can replace your mother's presence, but there are ways to help relieve the pain of loss. You may find some solace or re-establish the following:

Keep up with the traditions.

It can be difficult to start grieving a loss, but it is important to do so. While it may seem like the natural response to grieve is to go into isolation, it can be helpful to include some of your mother's favorite traditions in your life as you start to feel better.

For example, if she loved baking, you could bake her favorite desserts and share them with friends or family members. If she loved being outdoors, you could find a way to spend time outdoors in nature.

Whatever your mother's favorite activities were, find ways to incorporate them into your life as a way of coping with your grief. By including your mother's favorite traditions in your life, you will be able to stay connected to her even after she has passed away. Establishing your own traditions may provide you with comfort in knowing that your children will inherit both yours and your mother's traditions.

Prioritize happy memories.
When you are grieving the loss of your mother, it might be difficult to remember the good times. It's hard to think about how much she did for you and how she was always there for you.

It's important to remember the good times and cherish them. You might not be able to change the past, but you can change the future by remembering the good times and letting them help you move forward.

Check out more maternal figures.
Being a mother does not always imply a blood relationship. You may have had several mothers in your life. If you have lost your mother, seeking another mother's support can assist you in retaining her sense.

Find a woman who has been through a similar experience and offer her your time and your love. You will gain much needed comfort from her and you will be able to learn more about your own experiences.

Practice mindfulness.
Mindfulness is the ability to focus on the present moment rather than allowing thoughts to lead you down an emotional road. Sometimes life can be very tough.

We are constantly bombarded with thoughts of the past and future. It's important to remember to take a step back and focus on the present moment.

This can be difficult because it's easy to get caught up in the thoughts of our past or future. Try using mindfulness techniques such as meditation to help you focus on the present moment.

The death of a mother is always a difficult time for the family. The death of a mother can be a time to reflect on what your mother meant to you and what she has done for you. It's also important to remember that your mother would want you to have a good life and live your dreams.

In honor of your mother, it's important to respect her memory by honoring her life. You might pay tribute to her by donating to her favorite charity. Discovering purposeful methods to honor your mother might give you a sense of personal satisfaction.

Aid Others.
Many other people, both children and adults, have lost a parent. If you are in the process of mourning the loss of your mother, it is possible that you are going through a difficult time.

It's important to know that someone else is going through the same thing as you are, and it is possible that you could be an important part of their grief journey.

You can help by offering support to your loved one, even if they don't ask for it. You may also be able to offer support by talking about your own feelings and memories of your mother.

Get local and professional support.

It may feel as if nothing you do can relieve the pain of your mother's death. There are many reasons why people face this problem alone. The most common reason is that they don't know how to tell their partner, or they feel that their partner will not be supportive.

Some may be too embarrassed to talk about it with anyone else, or they may not want to burden their partner with the responsibility of helping them solve the problem.

However, there is no reason to face this problem alone. There are organizations and resources available to help people with this problem. One of these organizations is called "Loveisrespect."

This organization provides resources and support for individuals and couples who are struggling with healthy relationships. Local support groups, online chat forums, and mental health specialists can help you navigate the grieving process.

The American Psychological Association's Psychologist Finder can help you identify a grief recovery specialist.

If you have been experiencing significant grief for more than a year or are having difficulty accomplishing daily duties, speak with a therapist.

Chapter 8: Healing and Staying Connected

RECOVERING FROM A LOSS

While the loss is fresh, it feels as if you will have to feel that way forever, but you won't. If you allow yourself to truly grieve, you will most likely discover that your overwhelming sentiments will subside in the first few months following your mother's death.

Individuals in our society frequently believe that we can get through grief in a month and be done with it.

Even if we do not recognize such feelings, they are present and have an impact on our lives in various ways.

Too many people pressure us to go on with our lives too quickly after a severe loss. When someone is grieving, it's easy to get caught up in the whirlwind of life and forget that the person is going through a difficult time.

It's easy to feel like you need to go on with your life and resume your normal routine as soon as possible because you don't want to be a burden to others.

However, it's important to take your time when grieving. You should be able to grieve in your own way, and not be pressured by others.

In the long run, it will make the person feel better about themselves and will allow them to move on with their life more easily. We must be allowed to grieve, but we must also alter our expectations.

You will never be able to get over the loss of a loved one, but the painful feelings you are experiencing will reduce as you accept the loss.

While your terrible emotions will take precedence, there is much to learn from a loved one's death. Such as how lovely life and love truly are.

While the loss of a parent is often unavoidable in a child's life, this does not make the process any easier. Many individuals struggle to understand grief and, in particular, how long it will affect them.

It is important to remember that there is no set time frame for grief to end. It is important to talk about your feelings and share them with those around you. However, it is also important to be patient with yourself and allow time for yourself and your loved ones to heal.

There is no predetermined time frame for how long a parent grieves. It is not uncommon for the grieving process to last a year or more. Sorrow does not magically end following the loss of a loved one. Reminders frequently bring back the agony of loss.

A person in grief must deal with the emotional and life upheavals that result from the death of a loved one. Over time, the sadness may lessen but it is only natural to carry emotional feelings around the departed for many years.

Depression is typically the most severe and prolonged stage of mourning. Unfortunately, what really takes us out of our depression is finally allowing ourselves to experience our darkest despair.

Grief is a natural and common process that is experienced by many individuals. It can be difficult to understand, especially when it comes to how long it will affect you. Grief can be a long process, but there are steps that can help to make the process more manageable.

It is important to talk about your feelings and thoughts with someone who is able to provide a different perspective. It is also helpful to keep an activity list of things you enjoy doing. This will help you feel like you are still taking care of yourself during this difficult time. We reach a point where we can accept the loss, make some sense of it in our lives, and move on.

It is now well accepted that losing a parent permanently alters our lives. Losing a parent is among the most emotionally traumatic and universal of human situations.

It is especially difficult when you lose a parent since you cannot bear the thought of living your life without them at first, and some people deal with it by pretending it is not happening. With grief, it is not always easy to know when it will end.

Some people may feel a sense of relief after a few days or weeks and then again may feel overwhelming sadness and grief after a few months. It is important to remember that grief can be different for everyone.

STAYING CONNECTED

One of the most effective methods I have found to honor and connect with my mother has been to practice and embody the qualities she valued in her daily life and interactions.

She was a wonderful, loving, and giving parent, friend, sister, and wife. And, while I will never achieve her degree of kindness, love, and giving, making a conscious effort to embrace those principles more in my own life has brought me closer to her.

Consider what shines out in your mind when others talk about you. While there is no requirement to do anything on the birthday or death anniversary of a deceased loved one, doing something can become a soothing tradition that allows you to show your love and sorrow for them.

It does not have to be the same for each occasion. Allowing for change is always a smart idea because your grief develops and evolves with you throughout time.

If you are assisting someone who is bereaved, keep track of these important dates and honor them when they arrive. You could even tell them a tale about their loved one if you have one.

It is vital to understand that there are no guidelines about how to stay in touch with a loved one after they have died. How you wish to honor their life and legacy is entirely up to you and your preferences.

Every person is different in terms of how they choose to celebrate their birthday or death anniversary, as well as how they grieve. Mourning is a very personal experience, and only you can decide the specifics.

For many people, losing their mother is more difficult than losing their father. Not because they did not love them, but because the link between mother and child is unique. Your mother gave birth to you. Throughout your childhood, she fed and nursed you.

In most circumstances, the mother has the greater responsibility for the child's care and is at home with the children more than the father. No one is ever as interested in what you accomplish or as proud of you as your mother.

Even if you did not have the best relationship with your mother, her death might be equally heartbreaking. You no longer have the opportunity to make amends or to hear her say, "I love you or I am proud of you."

Although the loss of a parent is an inevitable part of growing up, it is no less traumatic. Many people, though, are startled by how much it impacts them. Their friends and family may not realize how devastating it might be, especially if they have been elderly or ill for a long time and their death was predicted.

Sorrow over the death of a mother is one of the most difficult things we confront in life, yet we all have to face it at some point. Everyone's sorrow is unique, and we all cope in different ways. We may experience some or all of the mourning emotions at times, or we may only experience sadness.

Be mindful that men and women grieve in various ways. Do not be too hard on your partner if he is unable to provide you with all of the assistance you require. That is a terrible moment for them as well, and no one knows what to do or say.

Know that you are not alone in your feelings. Speak with your friends and relatives. Attend a grief support group, but do not be ashamed to be sad. It is a natural and typical procedure that everyone goes through at some point in their lives.

Keep the following in mind as well: Be kind to yourself, since you are the source of your success and peace. Follow your instincts. Realize that no one can ever truly fill that gap in your life. Finally, remember that healing takes time, so be patient with yourself.

Chapter 9 - Grief Overload

Grief overload is what you feel when you experience too many significant losses all at once or in a relatively short period of time. The grief of "loss overload" differs from typical grief in that it stems from multiple losses and is jumbled.

Losing a mother is a pain that cannot be described in words. It is impossible to move on from the memory of losing the woman who sacrificed happiness in her own life so that you could have a better one.

A mother's love is truly irreplaceable, as it is a love that is both unconditional and unconditional. It is a love that never stops and does not require an explanation, but it is also one that can be completely explained. A mother's love has the ability to make us feel loved and cherished, even when we feel like we are not deserving of her love. A mother's love for her child is a love that will never end, no matter how old or grown up the child becomes.

If you are finding it hard to cope with your mother's death, channel your emotions by seeking solace in the written word. Write your own quotes, phrases, and poems. They will help you reflect on all the beautiful childhood memories.

"SOMEDAY"

"So dear was she
That any walking gear stand not with glee
It was another wrong sweep
Of that coward's rake
Hoped not to claim a fake

But the very best of our garden

On the worst moment of any hour

Had she made a will

Would have had it claimed still!

I well remember the advice you gave

Little not knowing I'll not behold you again

I still fight against losing bits

Of that angelic face

Which threatens to blur

A nine year old ace

Could death but have a reason to drive?

A look over these nine year dives

Through dawns of memories to save

Will jilt a shameful regret

For its unreasonable wave

This regardless arm of death

It's ever spinning wave

Of harvest on mother-earth.

Need to say, there is a bright line

One day to severe to enable us whine

A joy great enough to shade empty years

With overflowing joyful tears

And the embrace

So heavenly sweet and warm

Holding on forever

To let the lost years wane off."

#anavoshio

Your words will assist you in emerging from the shadows of grief. The lovely memories you have of spending time with your mother will help you heal from the sorrow of losing her after she has died.

"ANOTHER SAD SONG"

"It's been twenty-four years now

The vessel that brought us said goodbye

And over my pillow

Thinking I could die

I bled my eyes yet again

To the pains and the overly truth

The messenger in black

Had made a wrong sweep

Fearful and empty

Were the little we

Emptied before a harsh world

So unprepared for the rough ride

Knowing you'd left with

Regrets of a life unfulfilled

We'd picked up the brevity

Amidst the loneliness and grin chuckles

And the undeniable glimpse of you

Your light had kept us alive

Made men from boys

And will keep us aglow

Till we meet again

Adieu mother.

You were super."

#anavoshio

The pain of losing your mother is indescribable. We can only keep going and hope that one day we will feel better. The best way to cope with the pain of losing your mother is to take care of yourself and stay active. If you don't take care of yourself, it's easy to fall into a deep depression and become isolated from your friends and family. It's important to be around people who are positive and encouraging because those people are what make you feel better. That one day we will feel a little better. Our mothers would not want us to be depressed and unhappy every day. They would prefer that we live happy and full lives. My thoughts are with you everyone since I understand your situation.

Chapter 10 - The Conclusion

I adored my mother. Watching her do a lot of things so perfectly in my child's eye. She would alter the furniture arrangement in the house once every three months. Washing and wiping every corner of the house to make it sparkling. The kitchen pans, pots, and plates were not spared the ordeal.

She was a practicing nurse, so her neatness was not all assumed. From the moment she arrived from work to the moment she tucked us in for bed, we were her priority.

When the deviant appeared, she did not spare the rod either. She made sure I was tamed to obedience. That was Mother. Discipline and sound development enveloped us when we were growing up.

Mother would go to any length to ensure that I am well taken care of. It was no surprise that I was the only one who remembered her fondly while growing up in the Sabo, Iyakpi, and South-Ibie suburbs.

A lot of my life's decisions and executions were mounted on her daily manual. Doing the exact same things she would love to do. Growing up into a man, none of those fine memories were lost. I seem to vividly imagine having her watch me do a lot of things.

I would even console myself by asking for her approval before carrying out anything. Funny behavioural attitudes then, when I look back now. My relationships and eventual marriage over time did not escape seeking her approval, even if she was not physically present.

I will tell you why I adopted that method of conjuring up her memories. Many people with mothers do not really know the precious gift they have been given. I hope you can carry your mother's love like she would want you to.

"MAMA"

"Just alone a walk, a foot ever
Ahead the other as just alone I cried
Recalling those moments with mother
Of pleasantries she'd offered

I never thought round
That she could leave forever so
The form and void never to be found
So near my tender soul

It's not fair
Letting memories die to glee
To a gem so rare
And heavenly bound as was she."
#anavoshio

Her loss, though painful, can be softened by my honoring her attitude by doing what I know she always does. And that cools me off. You are her legacy. She is always with you.

Mothers will live on in us forever because they gave us life and safeguarded us. Mothers are always by our sides. Even if they are not present, they exist in us because we are them. This is my version of the "Lion King's Mufassa: He lives in you" song, and she now lives in you.

I am proud of my mother, and I know she is smiling down on me. The manual of discipline she left is intact. You will not have an unsettling realization when you conjure up emotional images of your mother—her bright, cheerful side. Sadness, tears, and urges to break down in grief will be highly muted. It is what your mother would have wanted.

You must live your life with the knowledge that they are happy for you. My siblings are now all married and have children too. They coped. They all threw themselves into diverse new adventures and came out successful.

Until they have lost a parent, no one can possibly grasp how this feels. The anguish and pain of loss caused by my mother's death have not gone away; they remain ever-present.

Most of the time, I put on my game face for the benefit of my younger siblings. I did not want people to believe I was crumbling. As a result, I kept a lot of my misery inside.

It is hard to fully grieve, especially when you are the eldest of the family. I would not dare break down before them. It would look too weak to make them carry on a memory of the boldest amongst them, who could not contain himself with the loss of their mother. Those were my motivations for taking risks in the face of adversity in my early years.

The first time I showed the pain and grief was in my boarding days at Onicha-Olona, a faraway town near Iselle-Uku in Delta state. Those rushing pangs of pain and grief from my struggling younger days have now subsided

Her sweet memories have always been my comfort in my afflicted hours. At times I felt like a child and thoroughly helpless, but I have been able to instill her loving memories into everything good I accomplish.

Imagine your mother sadly passing during the COVID pandemic. Alone in a hospital bed with no close relatives. Imagine the grace and dignity with which she must have fought to the end, hoping at the end that she would pull through to see you and your loved ones once again.

Consider a world in which she is no longer physically present, her distinct laughter and voice gone, forever. The pain that follows never leaves, and the grief is unbearable.

The emptiness you feel is indescribable. At times, when the pain of the loss hits me, I choke, unable to breathe. And I just have to come out to get a gulp of fresh air outside. You can beat it too.

Mothers are always present in us because they gave us life and safeguarded us. Even when they are not present, they live in us because they are us. This is always my comfort and padding when I examine periods past and present.

Sometime, I would wish us texted each other on my mother's birthday or the anniversary of her death, but none of these details are available to us, her children. Nobody seemed to bother letting us know.

Little is even known of my mother's father. Grandma had asked me not to bother him the last time I had a talk with her. And father had scared me off when I asked him if a certain name was my mother's father's name. He had asked me to get out of his face.

This bit me hard at that time. He did not hide his hatred for my mother's linage from a young me back then. I was so very young to be shouted at like that. And from someone you refer to as your father.

I was able to ask a brother of hers, and I was told she was born in 1955. The day and month, I suppose, will be lost forever now that everything about mother has died except for us, her legacy. I will thrive on passing on that feeling of love and awesomeness that my mother left me to my daughter so that she will know my mother's love. That way, our mother can actually live forever.

For those of you who still have your mothers around, you are blessed. Tell your mother you love her. Seek her advice and wisdom. Do not take these moments for granted. You only have one mother, and when she is gone, you will wish you had never said an ugly word to her your whole life.

"I WRITE TO HEAVEN"

"Dear mum,
There were times
I'd thought I heard my name

There were times I'd thought
I heard a voice I knew long silent

There were times
I'd lifted my head
Above my worries
And thought I saw you
Standing close to me
And with an aggrieved heart

Wanting to cry for the lost years
I'd shoved forward to grasp you
But you always had melted away like mist
Slipping through my fingers
Lifting up like smoke due for heaven

And I'd wished bitterly
That I could fly to the skies
To just sniff your whiff
Even to justify your actuality
I love you, mum.
#anavoshio"

Printed in Great Britain
by Amazon

19614662R00066